CRYPTOCURRENCY

"Virtual currencies, perhaps most notably Bitcoin, have captured the imagination of some, struck fear among others, and confused the heck out of the rest of us."

– US Senator, Thomas Carper

CRYPTOCURRENCY

The Beginner's Guide
To Investing and Trading in Cryptocurrency

E.C. Johnson

CRYPTOCURRENCY
The Beginner's Guide to Investing and Trading in Cryptocurrency

This document is geared towards providing exact and reliable information in regards to the topic and issue covered. The publication is sold with the idea that the publisher is not required to render accounting, officially permitted, or otherwise, qualified services. If advice is necessary, legal or professional, a practiced individual in the profession should be ordered.

- From a Declaration of Principles which was accepted and approved equally by a Committee of the American Bar Association and a Committee of Publishers and Associations.

The information provided herein is stated to be truthful and consistent, in that any liability, in terms of inattention or otherwise, by any usage or abuse of any policies, processes, or directions contained within is the solitary and utter responsibility of the recipient reader. Under no circumstances will any legal responsibility or blame be held against the publisher for any reparation, damages, or monetary loss due to the information herein, either directly or indirectly.

Respective authors own all copyrights not held by the publisher.

The information herein is offered for informational purposes solely, and is universal as so. The presentation of the information is without contract or any type of guarantee assurance.

The trademarks that are used are without any consent, and the publication of the trademark is without permission or backing by the trademark owner. All trademarks and brands within this book are for clarifying purposes only and are the owned by the owners themselves, not affiliated with this document.

The more that you read, the more things you will know.

The more that you learn, the more places you'll go.

- Dr. Seuss

Table of Contents

Introduction

Is money dead?

I know you didn't come here to discuss that. You are interested in the burgeoning world of Cryptocurrency, and the exciting, yet obscure, new ways to get rich from the Internet. You're enticed by the sexiness of Bitcoin, and the lesser known Ethereum. You doubt the traditional stock market, and you're interested in the exceptional returns of the virtual money market. So no, you don't care to discuss the teetering existence of our current barter and trade system. You picked up this book for one reason, and one reason only. To learn how to profit from Cryptocurrency.

You won't be disappointed.

With this book you will learn about the power of Cryptocurrency, and where it originated. You will be shown the huge potential of digital currency, and how to invest in it. And yes, you will also learn why the slow death of our most recent iteration of money will result in the boom of the virtual dollar. Are you ready?

Welcome to the world of Cryptocurrency

SECTION 1
UNDERSTANDING MONEY

Chapter 1: The Power of Money

A Tale of Money and Men

It is a warm summer morning in Charleston, SC. The sky is clear blue, and a gentle breeze plays off the nearby ocean. It's a beautiful day for a graduation. Roughly 1600 students mill around the college grounds, dressed in white and awaiting the ceremony. Their families are likely concerning themselves with how to bend the rules of street parking, and whether they arrived early enough to be seated in the majestic, oak-lined garden known as the Cistern, or if they will be re-directed to a nearby basketball stadium. It is a day of excitement, accomplishment and tranquil reflection. It also begins the 6-month countdown, for many graduates, to the moment when they must grapple with paying back crippling student loans.

Many of these optimistic graduates will be unemployed, or under employed by the time the loan's "grace-period" clock is up. They will be forced into unsatisfactory careers and begin working paycheck to paycheck, in order to pay the bills. They will work hard to accrue a form of currency becoming less valuable, and more obsolete. They treat money as a viable, necessary object rather than a malleable, economic tool. It is their lack of awareness which makes life that much more difficult.

And why is that? It's not as if money is a foreign concept or difficult to understand. In fact, money is something we all use, and it has a history almost as long as the history of the human race. To put it simply, money is any item(s) generally accepted as payment for goods, services and debts between two or more parties. The act of exchanging money is simply bartering, and we have been bartering as a species for years.

Thousands of years ago, shells, beads and grains were acceptable currencies in a bartering society. As technology became more advanced, and governments expanded their influence, money evolved in relevance and power. Today, much of the world's money is based upon a *Fiat* system where bank notes and coins are assigned value in accordance with the government they represent. In fact, the value assigned to a nation's money is linked more to that nation's influence than on tangible items, such as silver and gold. Money is as much political as it is economic.

During the American Civil War, the confederate states printed their own paper money in a show of defiance to the Union and to help legitimize their campaign. Once the Union won the war, however, the confederate bank notes were quickly put out of circulation.

Regardless of what type of bank note a person may hold, it is generally agreed that there are two main attributes of a successful currency. These features are:

(i) Utilizing money as a means of exchange
(ii) Using money to store and denote value

In order for money to fulfill these roles, the people who use the money must maintain a certain level of trust in the currency, and the entities who regulate it. This brings us back to my initial assertion that Money is dead. Or rather, the modern interpretation and control of *fiat* money, is dead.

As in the earlier example of the American Civil War, money becomes obsolete when it is no longer held as an acceptable form of currency. It cannot be exchanged for goods, services and debts; and the government backing it does not have sufficient influence to assign value. The general populace loses faith, and the money dies.

Now, let's turn our attention to what we consider contemporary fiat money. In the 1970s, the U.S. dollar was taken off the Gold Standard, with the economy itself being used as the barometer the government utilized to assign value. More money could be printed, and inflation could be manipulated to an even higher degree. With the advent of the Information Age, money became digital. What once could be buried in the back yard for safekeeping, or transported across territory lines via coach and wagon could now traverse miles and nations in a virtual blink. "Cash" money, became an inconvenience. It's too bulky to carry around large amounts; easily misplaced and more difficult to exchange for another currency.

Converting our modern money to a digital platform is the next logical progression. However, it also comes with virtual disadvantages. No, there aren't any Wild West outlaws saddling up to your local 'Western Union' and threatening to shoot up the town if not given a wire transfer. No, the villain is more ominous, and faceless. Every day, companies and banks are attacked by hackers and identity thieves whose goal is to reroute those monetary zeros and commas from one place to another. And what's worse, these virtual outlaws are outpacing the governments tasked with protecting money.

Established entities find it difficult to counteract these attacks and, instead, spend resources (i.e. - *your money*) to clean up the aftermath. This is in addition to the continual manipulation of money for political and economic gain. The public's trust in the value of modern currency, and its protection has been diminishing for some time now. People are ready for the next iteration of money. They want a faster, safer currency and one not so easily manipulated by the proverbial "talking heads." It was this progression of thought which led to the creation of Cryptocurrency.

What Is Cryptocurrency?

Cryptocurrency is money created by the use of encryption techniques of advanced computer programming. These same techniques are used to carry out and verify the transfer of funds. Cryptocurrencies are independent of central banks and are decentralized.

In 2009, Bitcoin became the first feasible Cryptocurrency, proving that a decentralized currency could exist, which is ironic, given that Bitcoin inventor, Satoshi Nakamoto, never set out to create a new form of money. He wanted to solve the problem of centralized digital cash and created a peer to peer digital cash system. He ended up developing Bitcoin, a totally unregulated form of currency which relied upon extensive mathematical computations to validate authenticity. It was with the birth of Bitcoin, that Cryptocurrency became a reality.

The implications of Cryptocurrency are so great that a number of central banks have attempted to involve themselves in the technology. However, the currency they produce is not officially considered Cryptocurrency as they can only develop centralized money. The proponents of Cryptocurrency are very keen on keeping the "true" digital currency decentralized.

Development of Cryptocurrencies

Cryptocurrency, such as Bitcoin, Ethereum, Litecoin and others, have had a lot of publicity. As the levels of financial/digital literacy of the general population has increased, Cryptocurrency acceptance has also made leaps in purchasing power. In 2010, a Bitcoin investor, known as Laslo, claimed to have purchased 2 pizzas for roughly 10,000 Bitcoins. It was considered the first instance where a Cryptocurrency was used to make a purchase. At the time, Bitcoins were virtually worthless. Today, Bitcoin is valued higher than gold, with 1 coin being worth more than $1500.

At first, most were very skeptical of Bitcoin and its technology, seeing it as a form of counterfeit or a device of criminals. This was particularly so when it was publicized as the means of trade on the 'Silk Road,' a part of the dark Internet where all sorts of unsavory behavior was rampant.

However, there is now an increasing involvement of legitimate business and government with Cryptocurrency.

As a consequence, the market capitalization of all cryptocurrencies is in excess of $110,000,000,000!

The Cryptocurrency Space

Midway through 2017, a check on the Internet revealed at least 900 cryptocurrencies. Most people have heard of Bitcoin, particularly as recent ransomware attacks have demanded payment in bitcoins. The benefit to criminals of this is that any such payment by a victim would be untraceable.

If the website for *coinmarketcap* is checked, it will be seen that there is a small graph beside type of Cryptocurrency, each showing the movement of the currency in the last week, as well as the percentage change in the last 24 hours. It will be seen that there is a great disparity in the values of the various cryptocurrencies with one Bitcoin being worth in excess of $2500 and a total market capitalization of more than $41,000,000,000 while a Cryptocurrency called Bytecoin was worth less than one cent although the total capitalization of Bytecoins was in excess of $386,000,000. Some cryptocurrencies have tiny capitalizations. An example is MikeTheMug Cryptocurrency with a capitalization of less than $200! We will have more to say about the quality and worth of cryptocurrencies later.

Cryptocurrency: Stocks and Fiat Currencies

The currencies we use, in everyday life, are called 'fiat' by the people involved in Cryptocurrency. Despite the word 'currency' in the word Cryptocurrency, there are greater similarities between cryptocurrencies and stocks than cryptocurrencies and fiat currencies. A purchase of some Cryptocurrency is a purchase of a technology stock, an entry in a digital ledger called a *blockchain*, and a part of the digital network for that Cryptocurrency.

Is Cryptocurrency Money?

The answer to this yes. Cryptocurrency is a means of exchange that uses cryptography so that transactions are secure and to exercise control over the manufacture of further units of the currency. Cryptocurrencies are a type of what is called alternative currencies.

Due to their frequent and great fluctuations in value, one of the two fundamentals of money, namely "a store of value" is lacking. Some digital currencies exhibit the behavior of countries having great inflation in that value is not retained.

Does Cryptocurrency Have Any Advantages Over Fiat Money?

It does and these were recognized when the first cryptocurrencies were designed.

1. Most cryptocurrencies are decentralized and are not controlled by any nation or business.

2. There is no central point of failure so if one organization mining bitcoins or other major cryptocurrencies fails then the currency continues.

3. The use of cryptocurrencies allows much greater privacy than the use of fiat currencies.

4. Cryptocurrencies are very easy to use, often much easier than fiat currencies which require time and fees for transactions.

5. Transfers using Cryptocurrency are much quicker than fiat.

6. For merchants, there is no danger of chargeback where a disgruntled customer can void a transaction that used credit card.

7. Due to its electronic form cryptocurrencies are far more durable and portable than fiat money.

8. As a result of cryptography, the chance of fraud is far less than fiat with credit card numbers routinely hacked and put on the Internet.

Computer Skills and Cryptocurrency

No particular computer skills are needed in order to invest in and trade cryptocurrencies. Having said that, there are great opportunities for those with quite typical computer skills.

One job advertised on the web recently was looking for a programmer with skills in PHP.

The advertisement read:

"xxxx is searching for people as staff for the position of PHP Programmer in a start-up company specializing in 3D printing and Cryptocurrency."

Another job on the freelancing site Upwork read as follows:

"We are looking for a super Cryptocurrency ninja to develop our most advanced and most power Cryptocurrency autotrading platform. It will be used to profit off of the price difference between many different currencies by constantly search the market for price changes and buy/sell accordingly to generate you a profit. Should be an easy work

for a Programmer/Developer Ninja.
We look forward to hear from you."

Hopefully, the person or persons placing the advertisement had better financial skills than skills in literacy.

SECTION 2
INVESTING AND TRADING

Chapter 2: How Do I Invest In Cryptocurrency?

Before any such question is answered, a more fundamental one might be, "Should I invest in Cryptocurrency?"

Cryptocurrency is the flavor of the month now. The value of Bitcoins has been rising for most of a year. In May 2017, Bitcoin reached $2,000 per coin and rose above $2,500 before declining to $2,400 a coin recently.

If those numbers don't impress you, then consider this: an investment in Bitcoin in 2010 of $100 worth, when each coin was valued at less than a cent would be worth more than $70 million now!

Even if you had purchased some bitcoin in 2016, you would very pleased. Bitcoin rose approximately 180% during that year. This compares very favorably with the stock market, whose returns ranged between 7.9% and 15%, according to reports.

Other cryptocurrencies beside bitcoin have also done well. As an example, *Ethereum*, which was launched during 2015, made spectacular gains including one gain of 35% in a 24 hour period. Another Cryptocurrency *Litecoin* is similar to Bitcoin but is much easier to obtain, easier to use, and regarded as having less value. This year it has gone up 700%!

Does this mean you should purchase Cryptocurrency as soon as possible? Some think so with some proponents expecting its value to keep rising. Some see a Bitcoin reaching a value of $100,000 within ten years. Although digital currencies may appear strange now, it is timely to remember that when Microsoft, Apple and other technology company brands began advancing in the 1980s, some believed there was no use for a personal computer. History has shown that these people were utterly wrong and people who were visionary enough to invest in Microsoft or Apple then are sitting pretty now.

However, caution and care should be exercised. If the price of an asset is going up, it does not mean its worth is truly increasing. Good examples are found throughout history with a particularly infamous one being U.S. real estate in the late 2000s. Often the things that are driving prices up are lies and exaggeration and if something goes up it generally comes down.

If you wish to purchase and trade Cryptocurrency, then you should first use the *exchanges*. These sites allow the acquisition and sale of Cryptocurrency with the use of fiat money. Before using an exchange you need to check how reliable it is and its quality. There are various ways of doing this which include liquidity, fees, limits for purchase and withdrawal, the volume of trades, spread, security, comprehensibility (user-friendliness) and fees.

In the previous paragraph, a number of terms were used. Some are almost self-evident while others are only meaningful to an investor. Let's quickly run through these terms:

Liquidity

This is the value of the coins that the exchange has. If an exchange has low liquidity, you may be unable to withdraw your coins.

Volume of trades

This is a term, which is reasonably straightforward. If the volume of trades is high, then the exchange has a lot of customers, which is an indication that they are in business for the long haul.

Spread

This is quite hard for the layperson to understand but generally, a high spread indicates greater difficulty in making a profit. Good exchanges will help you and advise you about this.

Security

This is another term that is hard for the layperson to understand. Good exchanges will help you and advise you about this.

Comprehensibility (user-friendly?)

This obviously refers to the helpfulness and user friendliness of exchanges. The online world can be very daunting if you do not really know what you are doing.

Cryptocurrency Exchanges

Here are a bunch of exchanges, where you can trade on cryptocurrencies. It is important that you realize that there are different trading rules for each exchange. For instance, certain exchanges do not even require you to sign up and create an account, while others require you to. If you decide to trade through different exchanges, it is important that you spot these differences and understand these rules properly before you invest heavily.

Some of the popular Cryptocurrency trading exchanges are as follows:

- Kraken
- ShapeShift

- Poloniex
- Bitfinex
- Coinbase
- Gemini
- Bitsquare

Most exchanges deal only with the big three cryptocurrencies which are Bitcoin, Ethereum and Litecoin.

If Coinbase is chosen, then first you must have a visa or master card that you have to verify yourself with Coinbase. Suppose you want to buy Bitcoins. The steps to buying Bitcoins using Coinbase are very user-friendly.

First, you click on Buy/Sell in the menu, if you are in a country that Coinbase does not support buys in you will be informed, you select Bitcoin, enter the amount you wish to purchase and follow instructions. You can see the Bitcoin you have purchased on what is called your dashboard.

At this stage, you can decide whether to leave your Bitcoin with Coinbase or send it to your *wallet*. We will have more to say about wallets in a future chapter.

Types of exchanges

These exchanges can be broadly classified into three types:

Trading Platforms:

These are websites, which help in connecting both buyers and sellers of cryptocurrencies. To facilitate this interaction, a fee is levied by these trading platforms.

Brokers:

These are websites, which you can visit to buy cryptocurrencies at a determined price. This price is determined by the broker. These brokers are similar to dealers in foreign exchange.

Direct Trading:

These websites provide a platform for buyers and sellers from different countries to trade and exchange currency.

Unlike the open market, these websites do not reflect the market price. Each seller has the option of setting his own exchange rate and trade. In other words, this platform provides the seller with a bit more flexibility while trading.

Tips before joining:

There are a few criteria that will help you choose the right exchange for trading purposes. Make sure that you pay attention to these, before you indulge in trading.

(i) **Reputation:**

The Internet has information about the different trading sites available. I have already listed the most popular trading websites above. You can choose from any of the sites above.

(ii)   **Fees:**

The owners of Cryptocurrency exchanges want to make a living and to do this they charge fees. These fees are usually a percentage of the trade and they vary greatly with some being twice as much as others.

(iii)   **Payment Methods:**

Each exchange has its own payment modalities. Check out the payment methods before you make up your mind. If an exchange has only limited payment options, you may not choose it because it might turn out to be inconvenient to use, at a later point in time. On the other hand, if the exchange offers multiple payment options, it increases the flexibility for making payments. Also, remember that a payment method can sometimes attract more fees. For instance, when you use a credit card to purchase cryptocurrencies, you will have to verify your identity first. You will also have to pay a higher transaction and processing fee. This is because there is an increased risk for fraud when you use your credit card for making payments on these exchanges. To safeguard you from that threat, a higher fee is being levied.

On the other hand, you will also have to keep in mind the time taken for completing the transaction, before choosing a payment method. As you know, wire transfer takes a bit of time. Hence, if you choose that as a payment option, it will take time, since the banks take their time to process these transfers.

(iv) **Geographical restrictions:**

Certain exchanges permit only individuals from certain countries to access and trade. Hence, make sure that you choose an exchange which does not restrict access and allows everyone across the globe to trade.

(v) **Verification requirements:**

Most exchanges in the UK and US require you to verify your identity before you can engage in trading. On the other hand, there are certain exchanges that let you stay anonymous and trade. While you might prefer to stay anonymous, I strongly suggest that you get the verification done. This will ensure that you don't get caught in any scams at a later point in time.

(vi) **Exchange rates:**

Each website has its own exchange rate. Before you decide on the exchange, make sure that you visit all these sites and look at their rates. Compare these rates and choose the one that is the most advantageous, keeping in mind the features that come along with that price.

Pros and Cons of exchanges

I have compiled the features, pros and cons of some of the popular websites that allow you to trade with cryptocurrencies. By having a glance at the below table, you will easily be able to identify those sites that are beginner friendly. I hope it will help you make an informed decision.

Website: Coinbase

Pros:

- It is one of the most popular trading websites.
- The fees requirements for this website are pretty reasonable, in comparison to other websites.
- It has a user friendly interface. Hence, as a beginner, you will not struggle to figure your way around this website.
- The currency that you store here is automatically covered by the website's insurance.
-

Cons:

- The customer service offered by this website is not as good as the other sites.
- This website supports only limited countries.

- This website has only limited payment options, which reduces your flexibility.
- The services rolled out by this website are not uniform across the globe. Hence, it might cause a bit of inconvenience if you are a frequent traveler and you wish to trade on the go.

Website: CEX.IO

Pros:

- It is one of the most popular trading websites.
- It has a user friendly interface. Hence, as a beginner, you will not struggle to figure your way around this website.
- You can easily access and trade from this site, using your mobile phones.
- It also supports usage of credit cards for making payments.
- The exchange rates offered by this website are reasonable, when compared to the other sites.
- It provides worldwide support.
-

Cons:

- The customer service/support offered by this website is not as good as the other sites.
- This website has an elaborate and long verification process. The long process can dissuade you easily from joining this site.

- Depositing funds in this website is expensive, when compared to other websites.

Website: Kracken

Pros:

- It is one of the most popular trading websites.

- The exchange rates offered by this website are reasonable, when compared to other sites.

- The deposit fee for this website is minimal, when compared to the other websites.

- The transaction costs associated with this website are also minimal, when compared to the other websites.

- The customer service/support provided by this website is excellent.

- This website has more features than most trading websites.

It provides worldwide support.

Cons:

- It does not have an interactive and intuitive user interface. Hence, as a beginner, you might find it difficult to navigate through this site.

- This website has only limited payment options, which reduces your flexibility.

Website: Shapeshift

Pros:
- It is one of the most popular trading websites.
- It has a user friendly interface. Hence, as a beginner, you will not struggle to figure your way around this website.
- The exchange rates offered by this website are reasonable, when compared to the other sites.
-

Cons:
- This site does not support fiat currencies.
- This website has only limited payment options, which reduces your flexibility.

The mobile application for this website is pretty average, when compared to the other sites.

Website: Bitstamp

Pros:
- It is one of the most popular trading websites.
- The transaction costs associated with this website are also minimal, when compared to the other websites.
- It provides worldwide support.
- It provides high security for your transactions and the currency stored in the website.
- This website is well suited for carrying out transactions in large volumes.
-

Cons:
- It does not have an interactive and intuitive user interface. Hence, as a beginner, you might find it difficult to navigate through this site.
- This website has only limited payment options, which reduces your flexibility.
- Depositing funds in this website is expensive, when compared to other websites.

Website: Poloniex

Pros:

- You will be able to create your account faster here, when compared to the other trading sites.

- This website is well suited for carrying out transactions in large volumes.

- The transaction costs associated with this website are minimal, when compared to the other websites.

- It has a user friendly interface. Hence, as a beginner, you will not struggle to figure your way around this website.

Cons:

- This site does not support fiat currencies.

- The customer service/support offered by this website is not as good as the other sites.

Website: CoinMama

Pros:

- It is one of the most popular trading websites.

- It has a user friendly interface. Hence, as a beginner, you will not struggle to figure your way around this website.

- Transactions can be carried out in a faster manner.

- It provides worldwide support.

- It provides multiple payment options.

-

Cons:

- The exchange rates offered by this website are higher, when compared to other sites.

- There is no function to sell Bitcoin.

- There is a premium that is being levied for usage of credit cards.

- The customer service/support offered by this website is not as good as the other sites.

Website: Bitsquare

Pros:
- It is one of the most popular trading websites.

- It provides a secure and private interface to transact.

- This website supports the trading of several types of cryptocurrencies.

- You don't have to create an account and sign up for trading.

- It provides worldwide support.

- The transaction costs associated with this website are also reasonable, when compared to the other websites.

-

Cons:
- The customer service/support offered by this website is not as good as the other sites.

- This website is well suited only for advanced traders.

- It does not have an interactive and intuitive user interface. Hence, as a beginner, you might find it difficult to navigate through this site.

- This website has only limited payment options, which reduces your flexibility.

Website: Gemini

Pros:

- It provides a highly secure interface for carrying out your transactions.

- This site provides you with analytics, which will helps you with your trading decisions.

- This website also provides higher liquidity.

- It has a user friendly interface. Hence, as a beginner, you will not struggle to figure your way around this website.

-

Cons:

- This website has only limited payment options, which reduces your flexibility.

- It supports trading of limited cryptocurrencies only.

- This website does not provide for margin trading.

- The customer service/support offered by this website is not as good as the other sites.

  This website supports only limited countries.

Website: LocalBitcoin

Pros:

- You don't have to create an account and sign up for trading.

- It has a user friendly interface. Hence, as a beginner, you will not struggle to figure your way around this website.

- It provides worldwide support.

- Transactions can be carried out in a fast manner here.

- It provides the user with multiple payment options.

-

Cons:

- The exchange rates offered by this website are higher, when compared to other sites.

- It will not be possible for you to buy Bitcoin in large quantities.

It supports only trading of Bitcoin.

When you have learned more about cryptocurrencies you may decide to trade. If you do, then a good place to trade is GDAX. There is no charge in moving your Cryptocurrency from Coinbase to GDAX.

With more experience, you may want to explore other more esoteric cryptocurrencies. This can be done at such exchanges as Bittrex and Poloniex.

You may be keen to learn more about trading. Do not rush in. Take your time. It is best to take it very slowly. It is best if you can find a real life person to take you through your first trades. There are YouTube tutorials on all aspects of trading, however, be careful as it is very easy to make mistakes and once you have lost Cryptocurrency it is gone for good!

Wallets for Cryptocurrency

Exchanges have their own wallets to retain the Cryptocurrency you have bought. Coinbase and other good exchanges have insurance to cover the possibility of the exchange suffering from a hack which leads to the loss of your Cryptocurrency. Such hacks have occurred and while your keys etc. will not be stolen, you may still prefer to store your money elsewhere. This is where 'wallets' become pertinent. We have much more to say about this soon.

Chapter 3: Do The Normal Rules Of Investment Apply?

If you go to Google or any other search engine and do research about investing you will get a lot of information, much of it very technical and difficult to understand.

The following comments on investment in cryptocurrencies are very useful.

It is possible to compare the growth in Cryptocurrency technology to the Internet boom in the late 1990s, however, some think it could be more. During 2016, the market capitalization of the total Cryptocurrency increased by more than 50% in about 6 months. The statistics on the growth of the top 100 cryptocurrencies are mouth-watering for an investor.

Often there are more to these Cryptocurrency projects than the transfer of digital currency, some of them add to or supplant existing processes with much better results. In the years to come, there will be a huge number of conventional and outmoded models which will be replaced by Cryptocurrency-based methods. Investors who are wise will try and decide those Cryptocurrency projects that satisfy a real need, and those which are nothing more than fads.

A Cryptocurrency Must Have Longevity

There are numerous rules you should obey when investing, with some of greater importance than others. The first is the rule of *longevity*. When selecting a long term investment, you must choose projects that have this, you must examine not only the product but those who produce it.

You must ask:

" Is this service going to be needed or utilized in the years ahead?"

" Is there any competition that will easily outdo this project?"

"Do the developers show commitment?"

If you find.

1. A current or developing demand for it,

2. no serious competition,

3. developers with commitment,

…then the project is worth considering.

A Good Cryptocurrency Project Provides Platforms Not Just Features

This is very important as a lot of the current Cryptocurrency projects are merely full of features, but don't offer a platform of significance. You may well ask what on Earth is meant by a platform. By platform, we mean a Cryptocurrency that has a number of different services. In other words, it does or facilitates something apart from being electronic money. Some cryptocurrencies are geared to a particular market such as betting or legal marijuana.

Today there are only 20 to 30 viable Cryptocurrency projects, meaning the remaining hundreds are of little use as investments with long-term prospects. Cryptocurrencies such as Bitcoin or Ethereum, with huge momentum and support, are platforms.

In assessing a Cryptocurrency, compare it to the large Cryptocurrency platforms like Bitcoin or Ethereum. Ask yourself does the project compare favorably? If it does not, then probably it is not a good long term investment.

Good Cash-Flow

Another criterion in assessing a Cryptocurrency project is the cash-flow. If you are looking for a passive income this is essential. Unfortunately, the success rate thus far for the majority of Cryptocurrency projects is not very good. The projection of future earnings and cash flows are problematic, as there is not very reliable information.

What Percentage of Your Investment Portfolio Should Cryptocurrency be?

This is very subjective and depends on a number of factors. Although Cryptocurrency has a lot of stories where people who only invested a little made fortunes, its volatility means that, to get the best results, you really have to manage your investments. Do not invest more than you can afford to lose, particularly if the whole world of investment is new to you. It is so easy to underestimate the risks posed by this volatility. Experiment with a small sum like $20 until you know what you're doing.

Here is a suggestion:

If you are less than 30 years old, then no more than 30% Cryptocurrency, with a good 50% in safe investments (don't hesitate to seek good advice about what is safe)

If you're in the age range 30 – 40 years old then no more than 20% Cryptocurrency and 60% in Traditional Investments

If you're older than 40 years old, then retirement should be a serious consideration and you should not have more than 10% Cryptocurrency, and you should have at least 70% in Traditional Investments

This is subject to many things like the job you have, the amount of experience you have in investing, your home situation, when you propose to retire etc.

Even inside your Cryptocurrency portfolio, you should have different coins, there are plenty to choose from. This process is called 'spreading your risk.' Never forget the old saying about not putting all your eggs in only one basket.

Chapter 4: Wallets

A Cryptocurrency 'wallet' is a secure container that is used for the storage, sending and reception of cryptocurrencies such as Bitcoin and Ethereum. The majority of cryptocurrencies possess an official wallet. For the better known there could be some third party wallets that are recommended officially. If you do not have a Cryptocurrency wallet, you will not be able to use Cryptocurrency. Wallets feature keys, which allow you and no one else to use them.

For any given coin, it is strongly recommended to use the official or at least an officially endorsed wallet. Be careful if you do not do this as some 'wallets' are nothing more than malware. Never use a wallet if you do not know or do not trust its source.

An important thing to understand about Cryptocurrency wallets is that they do not technically store your Cryptocurrency. Like physical wallets contain your actual money, Cryptocurrency wallets do not technically store the Cryptocurrency. Then why are they called wallets?

Cryptocurrency, unlike physical currency, does not exist at a single location anywhere in the physical or the virtual world. All that exists are the records of transfers. Therefore, Cryptocurrency wallets are more like ledgers of this Cryptocurrency for your account. That way, they know how much Cryptocurrency you have, and therefore enable easy transfers from your account or into it.

Keys of a Wallet

Every Cryptocurrency wallet will have two types of keys: a Private Key and a Public key. A private key is a completely secure digital code that is known only by you and accepted only by your wallet.

A public key is a key that corresponds to a certain value of Cryptocurrency. Public keys can be shared with the person you are trying to make a transaction with. The private key enables you to sign a personal message with the public key, which enables you to prove to the other party that you are the owner of the private key associated with the Cryptocurrency wallet.

It is important to note that the private key is fairly essential for keeping your Cryptocurrency account and the money inside it. You cannot share your private key with anyone.

Further, if you lose your private key, you lose your Cryptocurrency account. There are no ways to recover your Cryptocurrency account if you do not possess the private key. If you lose your key, all the money in your Cryptocurrency account is lost as well. Therefore, always keep your private key safe with caution.

Classification of Cryptocurrency Wallets

Do not think that Cryptocurrency and Cryptocurrency wallets will limit your choices and you have to use it a very specific way. The reality is quite the contrary. Cryptocurrency comes with a variety of options that increase the choices and flexibility that the service provides to you.

These wallets vary on the type of functionality, the online/offline mode, and the method through which the wallet is accessed. The major types of wallets are:

1. Desktop Wallet:

Desktop wallet is basically an application that is installed in the client's system. The clients can access the application through their desktop, and the application further makes communication with the online servers with the help of the Internet.

2. Mobile Wallet:

As smartphones are even more popular medium of communication and transactions than desktops, there are Cryptocurrency wallet applications that are designed for smartphones as well. These not only involve remote accessibility but also give the option of mobility.

3. Online Wallet:

An online wallet runs on the servers of the company that operate the wallet. It is a cloud based service. You can access it through a web browser of your mobile or desktop. These are secure services and allow secure transactions. The encryption and security level of online wallets is higher than desktops and smartphone wallets, if the online wallet is of reputed company. Otherwise, if the management of the online wallet is done by an organization, which lacks security or good synchronization, this method could act riskier than offline ones.

4. Hardware Wallet:

Hardware wallets are specific physical devices that are used for the purpose of safekeeping Cryptocurrencies. These devices could be a simple device like USB device used as a Cryptocurrency wallet. These devices provide the additional benefit of added security by acting as a physical key. When they are connected to a system, they can go online and access the Cryptocurrency servers. When transactions are done, they can be disconnected in which they go into an offline mode. Then they can be carried safely.

5. Paper Wallet:

Paper wallets act as a hardcopy key for accessing your Cryptocurrency. In case of paper wallets, the QR Code of your wallet is printed out on paper. Whenever you need to make a transaction, the QR code can be easily scanned by the system. You can send Cryptocurrency as well as receive it. Further, no data about your Cryptocurrency is stored in the paper wallet; it just contains a QR code. Hence, it improves security and functionality.

How Secure Are Cryptocurrency Wallets?

Security is variable. Some of the best wallets use bio information as well as other measures. One feature you can insist on is multi-signature transactions. As with all software, it is important to back it up. Encrypt your keys.

It's smart to backup your wallet and private keys and to encrypt them. You should have at least one backup on an external hard drive of some sort, preferably with no Internet connection so that you can retrieve them if you need to such as if your computer's hard drive is erased or you have another different disaster. If your wallet or your keys are lost then you can say goodbye to the currency within it! Generally, it is good practice never to have more currency in a digital wallet than one in daily life.

It is quite easy to transfer Cryptocurrency from an exchange to a hardware wallet. Here is an example using Coinbase and a hardware wallet called KeepKey:

1. The KeepKey USB cable is plugged in
2. The KeepKey Client is opened (on Google Chrome you will find it under Apps)

3. Locate the wallet address on the KeepKey Client User Interface

4. Access Coinbase 'Send/Request' tab and input your KeepKey wallet address. Click on Coinbase 'Send/Receive' and enter the KeepKey address when prompted.

5. Follow instructions then 'Send Funds' is clicked

It is always a good idea to send a small sum first to make sure all is working before you send the bulk of the money.

How to ensure the security of a Cryptocurrency Wallet?

While Cryptocurrency wallets are way more secure than traditional wallets, there are additional measures that you can take to make sure your Cryptocurrency is safe. These measures include:

1. Always keep your wallet backed up:

You should only store little amount of Cryptocurrency in your online wallets or desktop wallets. These wallets can be accessed by hackers and therefore might not prove to be a very secure medium for huge amount of Cryptocurrency. For big Cryptocurrency amounts, it is better to use a physical wallet or a paper wallet. These wallets act like a backup and work even if your computer drive's become corrupted or in case of theft of your computer.

2. Always keep your wallet up to date:

If your wallet uses any type of software interface, always make sure that you have that software updated regularly. Further, install the latest updates in your system as well. The updates ensure that any vulnerabilities or bugs in the system are fixed, that would otherwise have allowed the entry of hackers. Therefore, install the latest updates in your wallet software, your desktop operating system and the mobile operating systems.

3. Always have the maximum number of security layers:

As many security layers as there can be on a wallet, the better the wallet. Always ensure that you are using a Cryptocurrency wallet that is popular and known to be secure. Further, the password of your Cryptocurrency wallet should be strong and complex. Don't use simple passwords, guessable phrases about you, or dictionary words.

Further, make sure that your wallet has two factor authentication. This is an additional security measure that makes sure that even if someone steals your password, they cannot get inside your wallet. Further, additional pin requirements should be enabled as well, so external applications cannot access your wallet without your permissions.

Additionally, there are some wallets that offer an added functionality of multi signature authentication. These ensure that a transaction requires the signature of you as well as another user. This adds to the security level of the wallet.

Fees for Using Cryptocurrency Wallets

If you ask me, *is there any fee for using Cryptocurrency wallets*, the answer would not be that simple.

Generally, Cryptocurrency wallets charge no fees for storing your money. If you are using physical wallets, you would be charged some amount for purchasing the physical device or the token.

When doing transactions, there are a lot of people around the world (called miners) who employ their resources to keep a track of every bitcoin transaction and thereby keep the system running without errors. Therefore, for employing their time, these people need to be a paid a little bit per every transaction they track.

This amount can be set up by the user himself. There is no fixed amount that is charged for a transaction. Therefore, it would be up to you how much you want to pay. However, it should be noted that the more you set the transaction fee, the sooner your funds will get approved for transfer. Setting up a very low fees might mean that you need to wait longer (hours or even days) for your transaction to get approved.

Note that the transaction fee generally is negligible anyway. If the size of your transaction is 226 byte, on an average your transaction fee would amount to $0.12. Not very much, is it?

Some Popular Cryptocurrency Wallets

With a wide array of Cryptocurrency wallets available in the market, it can be a tough decision on which one you should choose. Further, it is important to consider that you should only put your money in a secure and popular brand. There might be many wallets that call themselves 'the best', but they could be simply a scam to lure you in and steal your Cryptocurrency.

Therefore, here are some popular Cryptocurrency wallets that you might want to use in order to safeguard your Cryptocurrency:

1. Ledger Nano S:

Ledger Nano S is a hardware wallet for your Cryptocurrency. On first look, it will look similar to a folding pen drive. However, the functionality of this simple looking gadget will amaze you.

The ledger Nano S will connect through your device with the help of a USB wire. In order to confirm any Cryptocurrency transaction, your Ledger Nano S must interact with the device. Further, this wallet can be used with tons of other services. It comes at a cost of around 58 euros.

2. Coinbase:

Coinbase is an online wallet that you can use for keeping your Cryptocurrency safe. It deals in bitcoins as well as ethereum. It offers its functionality in around thirty countries. It is not only an excellent wallet, but also among the top Cryptocurrency exchange services in the world.

3. TREZOR

Trezor is a multi Cryptocurrency wallet. It means that it can handle bitcoins as well as other sorts of popular cryptocurrencies. The wallet follows U2F Authentication protocol. Further, the platform has a tiny token that you can use as a wallet to store Cryptocurrency, as well as your own security key for the authentication of Cryptocurrency transaction.

4. StrongCoin:

StrongCoin is one of the oldest bitcoin wallets that are still in use today. It is a simple bitcoin wallet that can be used to store, receive, and send your bitcoins. However, as an added security measure, the private key of a user is encrypted in the user's browser itself before it reaches the servers of strongcoin. Therefore, ideally, no one but the user would have his private security key, not even the people at StrongCoin.

5. Ledger BLUE:

This is one of the premium products that you can use as a Cryptocurrency wallet to store your money in style. It is a physical Cryptocurrency wallet. It has an integrated touchscreen that you can use for smooth and added functionality through the hardware itself. Bluetooth is included in the product as well. Further, there is a battery that needs to be recharged. This works with many cryptocurrencies. Further, it can be used with other applications as well. This cool device will cost you around 230 euros, and will be available sometime in September.

SECTION 3
TIPS FOR CRYPTOCURRENCY

Chapter 5: Things to Watch Out For

Whether you look at Cryptocurrency as just an alternative transactional unit or as the next big thing in investment, you ought to be aware of the potential dangers and bad sides of this new kid on the block. So, let us see what we consider the most important downsides of transacting and investing in Cryptocurrency.

Absence of government regulation

Interventional economic regulation by the Government is akin to having a stern housekeeper. You hate it when they are there imposing conditions on you and giving you the occasional stern eye, but take them out of the house and you will end up realizing the absence of all the good that comes with a bit of regulation.

In case of Cryptocurrency, there is not a single international government that has established a comprehensive framework for regulation and monitoring of transacting in it. Some have let the individual organizations and users decide for themselves while some other governments have taken the extreme route of outright banning of transactions in Cryptocurrency. The perils of investing in Cryptocurrency of any form, in such a de-regulated climate, cannot be ignored.

Remember to wait until the transaction is approved

Cryptocurrency relies on the approval of a transaction to ensure that the money in really transferred. Therefore, if you are a seller, never act too hasty when a Cryptocurrency transaction is complete. Always wait for the approval no matter how much time it takes. The approval comes from the systems that are keeping track of all the Cryptocurrency there is; therefore it might take some time.

The approval for a transaction ensures that no duplication transaction is committed by the buyer. Since the transaction takes some time to get noted by a miner, if a buyer is using fast clicks it might be possible for him to duplication a transaction. Of course, the duplicate and fraudulent second transaction will get negated once the two identical transactions are received by a miner. However, if a seller has shipped the good before the approval of the second transaction, he might lose both his goods as well as his money.

Decentralization

Remember that Cryptocurrency is a much decentralized type of currency. There are no banks that have a hold of it, and it does not emanate from a single location. The currency depends on the thousands of people who keep their systems running all the time to keep a track of the transactions that are carried out in Cryptocurrency.

If you come in any sort of trouble pertaining to Cryptocurrency, you might go to help to a number of places but none of them might be liable to offer you a solution, since the currency is not centralized.

Security from cyber threats

Cryptocurrency is an entity that has taken shape solely on the digital landscape. And herein lies it's most endearing and dangerous attribute. This form of currency is the least protected from cybercrimes and hackers. You are there out on your own, when you decide to invest and hold on to Cryptocurrency.

Risks of your account being hacked into are high and, to make matters worse, conventional channels of dispute resolution are of no use.

Market value fluctuations

As mentioned earlier, the value of Cryptocurrency is not pegged directly to any specific market. But, that is not to say that it is free from value fluctuations. On the contrary, speculation based trading is indeed very high and value is often based on the perceived levels of acceptance of this currency. What this means is that your investment could lose half its value overnight without any concrete reasons to warrant that depreciation.

Moreover, in the United States, there are no governmental or federal insurance plans to cover your investments in a portfolio consisting of Cryptocurrency. Hence, in the aforementioned scenario of sudden depreciation in the value of your investments, you really have no safety net beneath you for recourse.

Taxation

In the United States, the IRS considers Cryptocurrency such as Bitcoin etc., as property for taxation purposes. Moreover, at present, this form of currency is not acceptable as a part of a tax qualified IRA. Hence, there are no legal solutions to shield it from being fully taxed.

Keeping Your Digital Codes Safe

Keeping your digital codes safe is another vital point if you are going to be involved in Cryptocurrency in any way. Your digital codes, be it your passwords, keys, etc. are like the opening key to your bank locker.

These can give someone access to all your fortune and hard work very easily. Therefore, it should be important to you that you take care of these digital codes carefully. It shouldn't be written out to the outside world so they can peek into it.

Further, in cases like your Cryptocurrency wallet, your private key is your only hope of accessing and making use of your Cryptocurrency. If you lose your private key, you cannot recover it and your account as well as the money inside it is lost.

Therefore, make sure that you have your digital codes securely with you, and you do not lose them in any case.

Cryptocurrency and the Darknet

If you are not familiar with darknet, darknet is the anonymous region of the Internet filled with all sort of content and markets that cannot operate legally and openly on the normal Internet that we access.

This darknet is accessed through secure proxies like the Tor browser. You can find everything imaginable on the darknet, no matter how much it is punishable by law.

The darknet hosts a lot of markets that deal with drugs, arms trafficking, etc. Since these markets wish to stay anonymous and untraceable from the law, all the transactions that are made there are made through Cryptocurrency.

Therefore, you need to ascertain that your Cryptocurrency account is not used for any such transactions. The law enforcement works hard in trying to catch up the people who operate these markets and the customers who reach out to these markets. Therefore, make sure that your account and its Cryptocurrency amount is only used for safe transactions.

Chapter 6: Tips for Getting Started with Cryptocurrency

In this chapter, I have compiled some tips to help you begin dealing with Cryptocurrency. As a beginner, it is important that you understand the concept well and plan your portfolio in such a way that you strike gold soon. Here are a handful of tips that can help you get there!

Ignore sources that are biased

When you decide to trade with Cryptocurrency, it is extremely important that you don't rely on biased sources for investing ideas. The minute you start browsing online for trading options, you will come across multiple sites promising good returns. As a beginner, it is extremely important that you stay away from phony sites, which offer surprisingly high returns. Seek advice only from reliable sources before you begin investing. Rely on your judgment and risk appetite and choose your portfolio accordingly. Do not get swayed by fake success stories posted on certain websites and make a hasty decision.

Start small

As a beginner, until you get a good grasp on how the market works, it is important that you do not exhaust your life savings at once. Start small. Keep aside a small portion of your income every month, for trading purposes. Invest small amounts at first and understand the nuances of the trading process. As you start making profit, slowly increase your investments. Do not make the mistake of investing huge sums, as soon as you experience a profit for the first time. Take your time to decide the optimal portfolio for your risk appetite. Once that is figured, you can gradually increase your investments.

Have realistic goals

Do not look at Cryptocurrency trading as an easy and quick way to become rich. As you already know, the Cryptocurrency market is highly dynamic and volatile. It will take you some time to get a grasp over the trading process. Hence, it is important that you have realistic goals, before you commence trading. Do not aspire to achieve a 25% growth on your portfolio immediately and then get disappointed if that does not happen. Have a realistic goal of starting with no loss, no profit scenario, when you begin trading. From there, move on to setting your growth rate at 5%, 10% etc. Have minimal expectations when you begin trading. This way, you will be able to study the market in a keen fashion and design your portfolio accordingly.

Don't try to guess and trade

Trading is not about making the right guesses. When it comes to an extremely volatile market, such as that of cryptocurrencies, it is not possible to sustain your returns, purely by making guesses. You might get lucky once or twice, but your guesses can only help you to a certain extent. You need to do your homework before you make an investing decision. Even if you are not a beginner, you cannot predict exactly how the market will react tomorrow. Make sure you keep an eye on the trends and watch out for market reports, before you invest. Despite all the homework, there is still a possibility of you not making a profit. However, one failure should not deter you from doing your homework.

Be patient and don't panic

When it comes to trading with cryptocurrencies, it is extremely important that you learn to be patient. As a beginner, you might make some trading mistakes. Or it might take you more time to understand the nuances of the market. Do not immediately give up on trading with cryptocurrencies, because of few mistakes. In fact, you will learn more from the mistakes, which will help you take informed decisions in the future. You must embrace the uncertainty element of the future and be prepared for the worst case scenario too. This way, you will not panic if you make a mistake or incur a loss. You will be able to regard at it as a short term phenomenon and try to come up with a strategy to overcome this.

When you learn to be patient, you will also cultivate the habit of reading the market carefully. When you read the market carefully, you will be able to take an informed decision. When that happens, the chances of you committing mistakes are minimal and the reasons to panic are also minimal. Hence, it all comes down to how patient and calm you are.

Learn from your mistakes

As I mentioned before, it is absolutely normal to make mistakes. These mistakes should not dissuade you from trading with cryptocurrencies. Given that the market for these cryptocurrencies is booming, it is only a matter of time and effort from your end before you make a tidy profit. Hence, it is absolutely important that you learn from your mistakes and correct your investing strategy accordingly. Your mistakes should be an opportunity for you to learn and better understand the market. Understand the root cause behind your mistake. Is it because you didn't do your research properly? Or is it because the market is currently a little unstable? If the mistake was within your control, you will be able to avoid it the next time. If the mistake/loss is because of market conditions and out of your control, you should stay low and wait until the market conditions improve. This applies to you, whether you are a beginner or an experienced trader.

Plan ahead

If you want to sustain your profits from trading, in the long run, you will have to come up with an investing plan. You can't aspire to make huge profits by just focusing on trading for the day, without keeping the future implications in mind. As I mentioned before, it is extremely important that you come up with an appropriate investing portfolio. This selection of the portfolio should be based on your goals, both short term and long term. For instance, if your desire is to make a return of 20% on your portfolio in the next 2 years, you need to plan out your investing strategies for the next few months. Of course, there is no assurance that your plan will work 100% at all times. But, at the same time, having a plan will provide you a sense of direction and help you invest wisely.

Now, if you are new to trading, it might be difficult for you to come up with an investing plan for the future, on your own. This is where you need to take that extra step and learn from others. Seek the advice of other experienced traders, study the market, watch out for trends and come up with your tentative plan. When you see that your plan is working, see how you can further improve it to optimize your returns. If your plan is not working, well, it is a lesson learnt! Remember, you can't just rely on others' counsel before investing. You need to do your bit of research as well to validate their counsel.

Don't trust others completely

When it comes to trading with cryptocurrencies, you are out there, on your own. You can't rely on the success stories of others alone and make your investing decisions. While it is extremely important that you seek the inputs of others, who are regular traders, you can't blindly rely on their trading advice. This is because a certain investing strategy or choice of investments might have worked for a certain individual at that point in time, due to various reasons. There is no reason for it to work that way for everyone. Hence, you should not be basing your investment decisions based on what worked for others.

In trading, it is important that you realize that there is no single solution to make profits. There is no one optimal portfolio combination, which can help everybody make profits. What is optimal for another individual depends on their risk appetite, goals, long term strategy, amount at disposal for investing etc. These aspects need not and will not be the same for each individual. Hence, it is important that you don't plan your investments only based on what others did.

As a beginner, you can seek the inputs of other traders with an aim of understanding the market better and how it works. You should go ahead and do your research to understand it for yourself. This is because the Cryptocurrency markets are highly evolving by the day. Since it is extremely dynamic, the modalities and market environment undergoes a lot of changes. You have to constantly update yourself and adjust your plan and strategy accordingly. You have to rely on your judgment before you make a choice. While a little distrust is good, it becomes a problem when you completely eliminate the idea of learning from others. Other traders may not be able to give you foolproof advice. But, you can most certainly learn from their mistakes and market conditions and tweak your portfolio accordingly.

Pick Currencies that have huge communities

With over 800 cryptocurrencies to date, you can be confused about which Cryptocurrency you should pick. If you want to invest in something new, do not go into a currency that no one has ever heard of.

Instead, choose a currency that has a good and established platform. The currency that you choose should have the support of a lot of community members. People should know about the currency. Having a community dedicated to a particular currency would mean that the currency is popular with the people, is stable and going to last.

Don't get bored

As a beginner, it is totally possible for you to get bored with the market. Unfortunately, the Cryptocurrency market is a little dry and difficult to understand at first. When you grasp the intricacies of the trade, you will learn to appreciate it better. You will be able to figure out matters of interest and come to love trading in due course. Until such time, it is important that you exercise patience and keep an open mind about trading. I know people who have given up too soon because they got bored with the market. If only had they stuck around, they would have made a good profit. Remember that the cryptocurrencies market is a tested and proven market. If you employ the right strategy, you will definitely be able to make good returns in the long run. Hence, when the boredom sets in, look at the big picture. That should dissuade you from giving up at the moment.

As I mentioned before, trading with cryptocurrencies is not an easy way to get rich fast. Hence, if you see that your returns are not doubling or tripling immediately, don't get bored with the market and underestimate its potential. Just trust your research and judgment and invest. You will reap good returns eventually.

Don't forget to have fun!

Do not look at trading as a mundane job or activity. At the same time, do not spend too much time overanalyzing the market. This will just ruin all the fun. You will forget to enjoy trading when you are submerged under market information. Learn to draw a line between being prudent and paranoid. When you are prudent, you will be willing to play around, have some fun and make money on the go. On the other hand, if you are paranoid, you will be thinking so much before making any investing decision. Time is of the essence, when it comes to trading. When the market is quickly changing, you can't forever question your decisions and lose out on the opportunity to make money. Enjoy trading. That way, you will learn more than you expected! With time, you will be able to develop a passion for trading. When that passion sets in, it is going to be an interesting journey for you!

These are just few illustrative tips to get you started. You will learn more, as each day goes, and this will help you customize your investing strategy accordingly. As I have already said, the keys to making good profits in the cryptocurrencies market are patience and knowledge. Build your knowledge base, bit by bit, and get rewarded in due course. Do not give up easily. This market is a gold mine, where only people who are patient and persistent strike gold. Hence, stick around, invest wisely and grow in the process. I hope you found these tips useful.

SECTION 4

FINAL WORDS

Conclusion

Congratulations! You made it through to the end! Not the end of your journey, mind you. That has only begun.

Always remember that the safety of your Cryptocurrency, your Cryptocurrency wallet, and everything associated with it is entirely up to you. This form of transactions is enabled for a more secure way of transferring currency across two parties, therefore always keep it so.

Cryptocurrencies have come a long way since they were first invented. A lot of security issues that were earlier present have been tackled with the advent of growing technology and better computer hardware.

However, there are still some issues that might be vulnerabilities to the system. These issues like the possibility of duplicate transactions or maybe anonymity can be hazardous to individuals as well as businesses, and therefore should be tackled as new technology emerges. Thousands of people are working on Cryptocurrency day and night to improve the functioning of the latest trend. If more people are attracted to the field, Cryptocurrency might just replace money as the ideal currency of the future. Maybe your grandkids would one day see a dollar bill falling out of your shelf and be amused by what is that? Sounds unimaginable? It might as well come true.

Cryptocurrencies are helpful and innovative way of digital fund transfer. However, many negative elements in the society use it for making illicit payments. Always forbid from using your Cryptocurrency for anything that is prohibited by laws in your country or international laws.

Always keep your passwords and keys securely with you. Do not share the private keys with anyone. The implications of this could be quite hazardous. All your money could be stolen, or even worse, used in an illegal manner.

With that said, using Cryptocurrency is like adjusting to the speed of the modern and the futuristic world. Cryptocurrencies are the way to transfer money in today's world. Not only it is secure, but the benefits are paramount.

Therefore, use it wisely and be a benefactor of its umpteenth benefits. Cryptocurrency can be an intelligent investment that may turn your fortune around. All you need is some smart skills.

Also, while diving into this Cryptocurrency world, you should do an in-depth research so you are well planned from the start. This book will serve as a perfect research source for you. Additional research can be done through the internet as well.

You should make up your mind about which Cryptocurrency do you wish to invest in. Which wallet do you want to use for you? What would be the purpose of the Cryptocurrency? Things like these should be clear in your mind, so you can take decisive steps.

Additionally, even if you do not really wish to invest in Cryptocurrency, there are many other ways related to Cryptocurrency through which you can make good money, without actually investing it.

As the cryptocurrency market is rapidly blooming, there is an increasing demand in the world for developers in the blockchain technology. Companies are asking for people who can design software, contracts, applications, etc. in this very field. If you know the basic science to program,

Cryptocurrency might be the birth of a career for you. If you are not familiar with Cryptocurrency programming, that is nothing to worry about. Many countries have institutions which provide courses in the same. And even if your country isn't among one of them, there are online platforms where you can enroll in online courses and be the best blockchain developer there is.

Further, the art of mining Cryptocurrency is on boom as well. People are calling it the next gold rush. You can make some space in your basement and start a Cryptocurrency mining facility with few resources. That might turn out to be a good way to make some money involving your hobby. You might even pool up with other people, so your chances of earning huge increase. Even corporations are participating in Cryptocurrency mining. Who knows, maybe one day you establish a corporation out of this.

Lastly, I have mentioned this time and again that Cryptocurrency is not like turning your fortune around overnight. You won't go to sleep one night and the next morning be a millionaire. It doesn't work like that. Cryptocurrency requires patience and a good use of your mind. Therefore, put smart work into the field and have patience. You are eventually but gradually going to profit.

Adhere to the values provided in this book. It can turn to your guiding way to success. Many people now are living an unimaginably good lifestyle due to the world of Cryptocurrency, and you could surely be one of them.

In the words of Nola Bushnell:

: "The critical ingredient is getting off your butt and doing something. It's as simple as that."

I wish you the best of luck on your Cryptocurrency journey. And with that, I will close this book.

Thank You for Reading…

E.C. Johnson

CPSIA information can be obtained
at www.ICGtesting.com
Printed in the USA
LVOW07s1354181217
560164LV00037B/2481/P